ANIMALS ATTACK!

Hippos

Diana Thistle Tremblay

KH

KIDHAVEN PRESS™

THOMSON

———— * ————™

GALE

San Diego • Detroit • New York • San Francisco • Cleveland
New Haven, Conn. • Waterville, Maine • London • Munich

THOMSON

---✶---™

GALE

Picture Credits:
Cover: © Frans Lanting/Minden Pictures
© Theo Allofs/CORBIS, 21
© CORBIS, 13
COREL Corporation, 18
© Alissa Crandall/CORBIS, 10
© William Dow/CORBIS, 37
© Peter Johnson/CORBIS, 26, 29, 33
Chris Jouan, 9, 17, 34
© Joe McDonald/CORBIS, 7, 31
PhotoDisc, 18 (inset), 23
© Reuters NewMedia Inc./CORBIS, 38
© Lynda Richardson/CORBIS, 25
© Jeffrey L. Rotman/CORBIS, 39
© Kevin Schafer/CORBIS, 14
© Skulls Unlimited International, 17 (inset)
© Bill Stormont/CORBIS, 5

© 2003 by KidHaven Press. KidHaven Press is an imprint of The Gale Group, Inc.,
a division of Thomson Learning, Inc.

KidHaven™ and Thomson Learning™ are trademarks used herein under license.

For more information, contact
KidHaven Press
27500 Drake Rd.
Farmington Hills, MI 48331-3535
Or you can visit our Internet site at http://www.gale.com

LIBRARY OF CONGRESS CATALOGING-IN-PUBLICATION DATA

Tremblay, Diana Thistle.
  Hippos / by Diana Thistle Tremblay.
    v. cm. — (Animals attack!)
Includes bibliographical references (p.).
Contents: Amphibious hippopotamus — Encounters on land — Encounters in
water — Living with hippos.
    ISBN 0-7377-1745-9 (hardback : alk. paper)
  1. Hippopotamus—Behavior—Juvenile literature. 2. Animals attack!—Juvenile
literature. [1. Hippopotamus. 2. Animals attack!] I. Title. II. Series.
  QL737.U57T66 2003
  599.63'5—dc21
                                                                    2003000875

Printed in China

Contents

Chapter 1

Amphibious Hippopotamus

A person on **safari** in Africa might expect to encounter some extremely dangerous wild animals, such as lions and crocodiles. Of all the dangerous animals in Africa, however, the animal that kills the most people every year is the hippopotamus. Hippos kill more people in Africa than do lions, elephants, and water buffalo combined.

Yet the hippo is not a predator. Most of the time, the hippo is a peaceful vegetarian. So why is the hippo such a danger to humans?

A hippo will attack to protect its territory and to protect its young. It may also attack when startled, **provoked**, or threatened. Sometimes, a hippo will attack for no apparent reason. One reason that hippos are so dangerous is that it is hard to predict what they will do.

Hippopotamus Amphibius

The proper name for the common hippopotamus is *Hippopotamus amphibius*. As its name suggests, the hippopotamus is **amphibious**. It lives both in the water and on land.

Hippos are unpredictable animals. Here, an angry hippo rears its head toward the camera.

A hippo rests in the water much of the day. After sunset, it comes out to feed on the African grasses. It returns to the water by dawn.

Most hippo attacks occur in the water, since this is where hippos spend their days.

Hippo Weapons

Although the hippo is not a predator, it is well equipped for fighting off predators such as lions and crocodiles. The hippo's size is a good reason for other animals to leave it alone. Hippos are **formidable**. An average male hippo is fourteen feet long, stands five feet high at the shoulder, and weighs three tons. The hippo is the second largest land animal, second only to the elephant.

A Big Mouth

A mature male hippo can open its jaws four feet wide. Inside these powerful jaws are many teeth, including four **canine** teeth that keep growing as long as the hippo lives. The two lower canine teeth are tusks that can be over eighteen inches long. The upper and lower canine teeth rub together when the hippo opens its mouth. This action keeps the tusks sharp.

To ward off attackers, the hippo opens its jaws wide and shows its teeth. If this does not scare off an attacker, the hippo may squeal. The hippo squeals so loudly that the sound can be heard for several miles. A hippo may also strike without any sort of warning.

A hippo's sharp canine teeth help to ward off predators.

On land, the hippo's speed makes it especially dangerous. Despite its bulk, the hippo is a fast runner. A hippo can run over eighteen miles an hour, fast enough to outrun most people. (The fastest runner at the Atlanta Olympics in 1996 ran about twenty-three miles per hour in the two-hundred-meter race.)

Hippos are also more agile than they look. They can make sharp turns at high speed. They can also run up steep hills.

Provoking a Hippo

Few people would be foolish enough to annoy a hippo deliberately. However, it can take very little to provoke a hippo. On land, for example, people have been attacked simply because they were in the hippo's way as it returned to the water.

Sometimes people in a boat bump into a hippo before they realize that the hippo is there. A hippo can be hard to see in the water. Its eyes, ears, and nostrils are all on the top of its head. The hippo can come up for air and barely show above the water.

The hippo sleeps in the water and rises to the surface every few minutes to take a breath. It does this without waking up, much as people roll over in their sleep. Sometimes a rising hippo bumps into a boat. Then the hippo is likely to attack the boat in a rage. If the people in the boat escape the hippo, they still risk death from drowning or from crocodile attack.

Hippo Territory: Enter at Your Own Risk

Hippos live in groups, or herds. A herd could be as small as two hippos. In a large body of water, a herd could have over one hundred hippos. The average herd has about a dozen members.

Each herd stays in its own territory. A hippo territory includes a stretch of both the water and shorefront. An average territory would be fifty or one hundred yards of a river, for example.

One older male hippo controls the group's territory. This hippo is the **dominant male** of the group. Other males are allowed in the group as long as they

How Big Is a Hippo's Mouth?

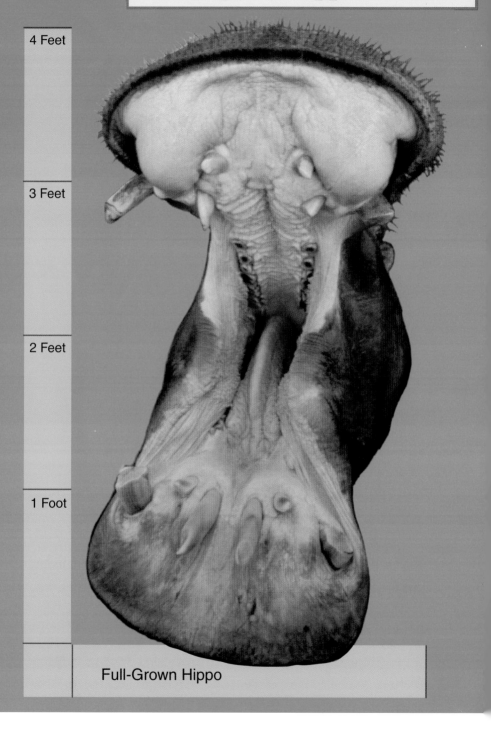

4 Feet

3 Feet

2 Feet

1 Foot

Full-Grown Hippo

A dominant male hippo defends his territory by threatening an attack.

submit to the dominant hippo and do not try to mate with the females in the group.

The dominant male is **territorial**. Trespassers are not welcome. To defend his territory, the dominant male threatens or attacks intruders.

Rogue Hippos

The most dangerous male hippo is a **rogue** hippo. When a male hippo is not part of a group, he becomes a rogue hippo. Rogues live alone.

Most rogue hippos are older males who have lost their territory to a younger and stronger male. They must establish their own territory away from other hippos.

Rogues tend to be grouchy. They might be insecure about their territory, ill, or lonely. Their bad temper makes rogues particularly dangerous. They are likely to attack any boat or canoe that comes into their territory.

Protective Females and Deadly Mothers

A female hippo with a calf is just as dangerous as a rogue. Female hippos are extremely protective of their young. A female hippo attacks anything that she sees as a possible threat to a baby hippo. This can include anything that gets near the baby or that comes between the mother and the calf.

For example, a baby hippo on its own is tempting prey for a crocodile. But if the mother hippo is nearby, the crocodile is unlikely to attack. A hippo's jaws are wide enough and powerful enough to bite a ten-foot crocodile in half.

Hippo attacks happen where hippo territory and humans overlap: the waters and grasslands of Africa.

Chapter 1

Encounters in Water

Most hippo attacks happen when people venture into hippos' water territory. Residents of an area are sometimes attacked while fishing or traveling by boat.

People on safari also risk hippo attacks. An experienced safari guide can take safety precautions to avoid attacks. Most of the time, the safaris are able to travel past hippos without injury. Yet many safaris are attacked, despite the skill of the guides.

The job of a safari guide is extremely dangerous because guides spend so much time in hippo territory. Many safari guides carry a gun in case of hippo attack. However, simply carrying a gun does not guarantee safety.

Rogue on the Move

One of the largest hippo **habitats** is the Zambezi River in southeastern Africa. It is also used by guides who canoe tourists down the river.

Every year on the Zambezi River, hippos tip boats, and bite and kill people. Yet guides still bring interested tourists on this dangerous journey. In 1996, Paul Templer was twenty-seven years old and living his dream as a canoe safari guide. Paul was well

A hippo capsizes a canoe on the Zambezi River in this 1866 drawing.

A juvenile hippo emerges from a plant-covered pool, ready to attack.

aware of the dangers from hippos and crocodiles. He carried a revolver in a holster on his belt.

Paul and the other canoe guides knew there was a rogue hippo nearby. The hippo had chased and bumped many of the guides' boats. They all knew where the rogue lived, so they avoided that area.

On this particular trip, however, the rogue had moved. When Paul and his helpers took out a group of six tourists, they unknowingly headed straight for the hippo's new territory.

Headfirst into the Hippo

As the canoes entered a large pool, Paul rapped his canoe with his paddle. It was his custom to do this to encourage any hidden hippos to surface. Then the paddlers could see and avoid the hippos.

Suddenly there was a noise like a thunderclap. A hippo hit the last canoe and threw it three feet into the air. The two tourists were still in the canoe, but Evans, another guide, was thrown into the water.

Paul paddled back toward Evans, hoping to pull him into the canoe. Evans reached out his hand to meet Paul's. Their fingers were just inches apart when the hippo exploded out of the water and roared. The hippo snatched Paul right out of the canoe. He took Paul's head into his mouth and dragged him twelve feet underwater.

"Where Am I?"

The hippo attacked so suddenly that Paul did not know where he was at first. "Darkness. Where am I?

Disoriented, unable to see, the only sense was touch. Tusks bore through my shoulders. I'm in a hippo! I started fighting for all I was worth."[1]

The hippo released its jaws. Paul got one arm free. He reached around and pushed on the hippo's snout. The other arm came free. As he pushed off from the hippo's lip, the hippo tried to bite him. The hippo's teeth scraped Paul's cheeks and the back of his head.

When Paul reached the surface, he was close to Evans. Evans was treading water, but he seemed to be in shock. Although Paul was hurt and bleeding, he cradled Evans's head in his bloody arm and pulled him toward shore.

Then the hippo was back. This time it grabbed Paul by the foot and pulled him under. Paul kicked with his other leg and beat the hippo on the snout. After a few moments, the hippo let go.

A Third Attack

Paul surfaced again. One of his helpers started to paddle toward him.

The hippo got there first. This time it grabbed Paul by the middle. His head and shoulders hung out one side of the hippo's mouth, his legs out the other. The angry hippo started to dunk Paul in and out of the water.

Paul's left arm was pinned between the hippo's teeth, but his right arm was free. Somehow he got his gun out, but the hippo ate it. Paul was running out of breath. He kept on hitting the hippo with his free hand.

Eyes, ears, and nostrils located on top of the head allow hippos to see, hear, and breathe while underwater. In addition, ears and nostrils automatically close underwater, letting hippos walk along the bottom of lakes and rivers.

Largest mouth of any land mammal.

Strong, stout limbs for running up to 30 mph.

Thick layer of blubber beneath the skin helps control body temperature, allowing hippos to remain underwater during all kinds of weather.

Rows of broad, flat molars for chomping up to 150 pounds of grass and leaves a day. Huge, tusk-like canines for protection.

Finally, the hippo rose to the surface and threw Paul into the air. One of the guides pulled Paul in from the water. They took him down the river by canoe to the landing spot.

By coincidence, the local medical rescue team was doing an emergency drill at the landing spot. They rushed Paul to the hospital. After a seven-hour operation, Paul was safe, but his left arm had to be amputated.

Fishermen prepare their nets on the Zambezi River. Rogue hippos (inset) pose a serious threat to anyone who enters their territory.

Going Back

Two years later, Paul, equipped with a **prosthetic** arm, started another adventure down the Zambezi River. This time, he was the head of a team raising money to provide prosthetic limbs to others in Africa who have lost arms or legs.

An important part of the trip was Paul's return to the spot where the hippo attacked. The other team members looked on as Paul made his peace with the river. One team member commented, "He is not bitter about what happened. He has said many times, 'I was the one who came into the hippo's home; he's been there longer than I.'"[2] And as far as anyone knows, the rogue hippo is there still.

A Well-Placed Oar

When a human and a hippo come into conflict, sometimes the human loses and sometimes the hippo loses. Either way, the result can be tragic.

Richard Bangs wanted an adventure in the wilderness. So he joined a safari as a raft guide. The group traveled down two rivers in Tanzania, in the largest uninhabited game reserve in the world.

As the group floated farther into the wilderness, they entered deeper into hippo territory. On the fourth day, they counted four hundred hippos. As the rafts passed by, the hippos reared up, bellowed, and stretched their mouths wide enough to swallow a man whole.

Richard's raft entered a still, calm part of the river. He was singing as he pulled the oars.

Then the raft reared up. Air hissed out from a puncture in one of the air chambers in the raft. The hissing stopped. Suddenly everything was quiet. Then, Richard reports,

> the attacker emerged—a great gray hulk, water washing from its head like off a whale's back. Tiny, turreted eyes flared as its mouth stretched like a steam shovel with teeth. It lunged, and instinctively I lifted the ten-foot oar and jabbed its blade into the fleshy, saliva-rimmed maw [mouth]. The animal bit the oar, twisted, then as I pushed the blade as far into its throat as I could, it let out a bellow then sank into the depths, leaving just a swirl on the surface as its signature.[3]

Slimed by a Hippo

That evening, the adventurers patched the punctured raft. The next afternoon, they had their second close encounter with a hippo.

The hippo surfaced just inches behind one of the boats. It shook its head and bellowed. "Paddle very hard!"[4] the guide screamed to his crew. They escaped to the bank of the river, where they found that the back of the guide's shirt was coated with hippo mucus.

The next afternoon brought the third and final close encounter. The rafts were bumping downstream in a fast current. Richard's raft was in the back.

Thick mucus drips from this hippo's gaping mouth.

A large hippo entered the river from the left bank. The previous boats had disturbed the hippo. It splashed into the river, heading for the safety of deeper water.

Richard realized that the hippo's path would cross his own path. Although Richard rowed as hard as he could, he could barely keep ahead of the frightened hippo. "At the head of the **channel** I was in front, barely, and glanced over my shoulder to see the hippo just three feet from the stern, his giant jaws clacking like some industrial shovel."[5]

A Thunderous Crack

Richard pulled for his life on the oars, but the raft stuck on a rock. "Brace!"[6] he yelled to his crew. Then he heard and felt a thunderous crack.

Richard thought that the hippo had struck the boat. But he turned to see another guide at the back of the boat, lowering a rifle. "In a boil of crimson and russet water, the hippo, with a hole between its stunned eyes, rolled and sank."[7] The hippo had come so close to the boat that the guide felt he had to kill it to save their lives.

Richard was shocked by the hippo's death. He explained:

Up to this point, the close encounters with hippos had been almost theme-park-like adventures; they popped in and out of our lives and sent our blood racing. Now, though, a line had been crossed, a life lost. The hippo, a gentle giant in

Although hippos usually avoid people, they will attack if provoked.

most scenarios, a vegetarian who keeps to himself, was only trying to escape perceived danger into the protection of deep water—and we had stilled him, for the sake of our little escapade.[8]

Richard says of Africa, "Survival of the fittest is more evident here than almost anywhere else."[9] When a person enters the watery territory of a hippo, it can be a question of which one will survive the encounter and which one will lose or even die. It is sad, but it is the way of survival.

Chapter 3

Encounters on Land

During the day, hippos seldom venture onto land except to lie together on the shore if nothing is around to disturb them. When people encounter hippos on land, it generally happens between dusk and dawn. Hippos come out of the water to graze for five or six hours every night. They start out after dusk and return to water by dawn.

The hippos follow the same paths every day. They trample the grasses to the ground, making a wide path. Someone who is close to a hippo path near dusk or dawn can surprise a hippo. This is how many hippo attacks occur.

If a person surprises a hippo, the hippo will attack if it decides that the person is a threat. This decision can depend on several factors. How close is the person? How much noise and movement is the person making? Is the person directly in the hippo's path? Is the hippo a female with a calf? There is also the unpredictability factor: What sort of mood is the hippo in today?

A hippo and a crocodile square off at the edge of a river. Hippos venture on land in search of food.

Tourists keep a safe distance while observing a herd of hippos. Attacks often occur when people venture into hippo territory.

Sometimes a hippo will stray from its usual habitat. Such hippos may be attracted by a farmer's crop in a field and make nightly visits to feed there. This presents two problems to the community: how to protect people and how to protect crops.

An Upset Easel

In Malawi, a country in southern Africa, an artist set up her easel near a river just before dawn. She began to paint the river scene. She glanced up from her painting to see a hippo running toward her.

Her first thought was how peculiar it was that she had not heard the hippo approaching. She wrote:

Utterly soundless! After the first timeless moment while I recognized this illogical fact—that this ton of outsized bath-toy was moving swiftly over leaf-littered and twig-bestrewn baked African earth without a single noise—came a second breathless moment when I realized that if I didn't move the hippo would pass within spitting distance of me. And I don't spit very far.[10]

Fortunately, the artist remembered that hippos cannot climb trees. She waited until the hippo was hidden behind a bush for a moment. Then she jumped up and ran behind the nearest tree, ready to climb up. She listened as hard as she could, but she could not hear the hippo.

Finally, she got up the nerve to peek around the tree trunk. She saw "a vast purplish rump vanishing through distant shrubbery in undignified but still silent haste."[11] She decided that the hippo was probably just as startled as she was!

"It Was Terrifying"

In June 2001, an angry mother hippo surprised a couple of tourists from Spain who were visiting Zimbabwe, a country in southern Africa. Jordi Mesdre and his friend were walking to their hotel just after midnight. They saw a mother hippo and her calf. They paused and waited for the hippos to cross the path. But the hippos stopped to graze about twelve yards in front of them.

Jordi was in front. He started to back away, toward his friend. The mother hippo noticed him, charged, and attacked. Jordi fell to the ground and scrambled backward on his back, beating off the hippo with his hands and feet. He managed to escape after a few yards, with bruises on his legs and arms from the hippo's teeth.

Later, Jordi explained that he was afraid the hippo would trample him if he screamed. "It was terrifying, but after falling I could only try to fend off the beast, and I consciously did not scream in fear of **aggravating** it." [12]

Jordi was wise to stay quiet. He was also lucky that the mother hippo did not kill him. She probably decided that he was not a serious threat and stopped the attack. She rejoined her calf, and they continued on their way.

From now on, Jordi said, he will look at wild animals only in the zoo.

Husband Attacks Hippo

A hippo charge is often fatal—but not always, especially when people use their heads.

One day in Hazyview, South Africa, Jamaica Mkombe was walking home from a church social with his wife, his pastor, and his pastor's wife. They

A large herd of hippos stands at the water's edge. Hippos occasionally come on shore to relax in the sun.

saw hippos in the distance, but they did not think the hippos would bother them. To their surprise, one of the hippos charged. It pinned Jamaica's wife against a tree.

Jamaica was carrying his Bible, his cell phone, and his shoes. He threw them all down and attacked the hippo with his bare fists. He drew the hippo's attention away from his wife. The hippo chased Jamaica for a short distance. Then the hippo returned to Jamaica's wife. Three times Jamaica attacked the hippo, and three times the hippo went after his wife.

Finally, Jamaica got the hippo to chase him toward a forked tree. Jamaica jumped through the fork of the tree. The hippo ran straight into the tree and stunned itself. When it recovered, it left.

Jamaica and his pastor carried Jamaica's wife home. Neighbors called an ambulance. The doctors said she was lucky not to have died from loss of blood. She survived with a broken arm and some broken ribs.

This was the second time Jamaica had rescued someone from a hippo. A few years earlier, Jamaica saved a six-year-old boy who was charged by a hippo.

Angry Mother Hippo

Tourists who visit locations where they can view wild animals such as hippos often do not know enough about animal behavior. This can result in tragedy.

On February 2, 2002, a South African woman was vacationing with her family in a national park in South Africa. She took her video camera onto the golf course and walked down to the shore of the river. She stood on the shore and started to film a crocodile in the distance. Judging from her videotape, she did not realize that a mother hippo and her calf were nearby.

The woman swung the camera around in the direction of the calf. The mother hippo must have felt this was a threat. She charged the woman immediately and bit her savagely in the stomach, the arms and legs, and the head. The bite wound to the stomach was so severe that the woman died on the way to the hospital.

A mother hippo keeps a watchful eye as her calf attempts to walk.

The park refused to kill the hippo because, they said, the hippo was defending her young calf. The park did put up an electric fence around the area where the attack occurred, however. The park officials also realized that the hippo population had grown too large, so that some of the hippos were venturing outside their usual range. They moved some of the hippos to solve the overcrowding.

When hippos attack people on land, the country's government needs to take action to keep its people safe. Sometimes the government decides to kill the hippos that are causing trouble. Creative solutions like fencing and relocation help keep people safe while preserving the hippos.

Chapter 4

Dealing with Hippos

People and hippos share a need for water. They both prefer to live near a lake or river with some level land beside the shore. Since people and hippos share some territory, people need to find ways to keep themselves safe from hippo attacks.

Safari Safety

Most hippo attacks can be avoided. Tourists in Africa can increase their safety by carefully choosing their lodge and their safari guide. Some lodges in Africa send out armed guards to accompany their guests on land. After dark, guests are advised to remain indoors.

If a person encounters a hippo on land, it is best to retreat while looking for a tree to climb if necessary. Since hippos cannot jump, a person could make use of an obstacle such as a fallen tree.

Out on the water, the wise tourist goes with an experienced safari guide who knows the hippo territories. The guide will keep the boat or canoe in the shallow water. The hippos prefer the deeper water, especially as hiding spots if they have been disturbed.

People who stay calm and quiet in an attack seem to do better than those who panic. Making a lot of

A photographer takes pictures of a hippo herd. Tourists must be very careful when approaching hippos.

noise and commotion is likely to attract the hippo's attention and may irritate the animal into a further attack.

Staying Calm

The best way to avoid a hippo attack is simply to avoid hippos. That is not always possible, especially for a professional crocodile hunter like Brian Dempster.

One night Brian was in a boat on the Zambezi River, hunting crocodiles by flashlight. He had two native African assistants with him.

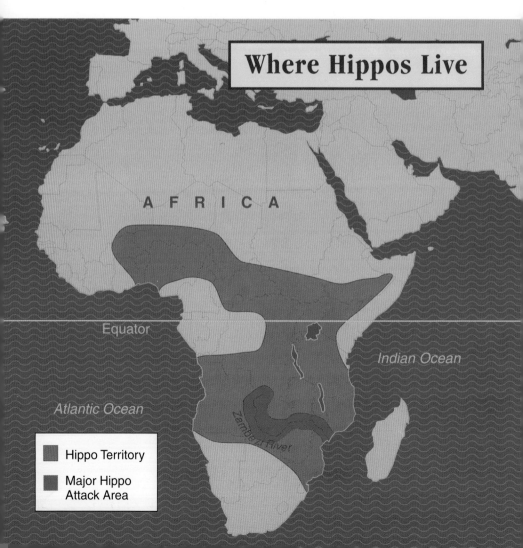

Where Hippos Live

AFRICA

Equator

Indian Ocean

Atlantic Ocean

Zambezi River

Hippo Territory

Major Hippo
Attack Area

Just before dawn, they were heading back toward camp in their boat. Without any warning, a huge hippo rose up from under their boat and threw it into the air. Then the hippo attacked the empty boat in a rage. It crushed the boat with its teeth, biting and tearing at it until it sank.

Brian was treading water nearby. He began to paddle very gently toward shore, trying not to make too much commotion.

One of Brian's helpers splashed wildly close by. "Help me!" he cried. "I cannot swim!"[13] The furious hippo turned from the remains of the boat and went underwater. It exploded out of the water right next to the splashing man, dragged him underwater, and killed him.

The second helper copied Brian's strategy of swimming calmly, and they both made it to shore.

Dangerous Filming

Years of experience filming wildlife does not protect a person from hippo attack, as filmmaking team Alan and Joan Root discovered. They were filming underwater at Mzima Springs. Mzima Springs is a pool of natural springwater in one of Kenya's national parks. It is a popular watering hole for animals and is home to many creatures, including hippos.

One of the male hippos had just lost a battle with another male hippo. He came across Joan with her camera and lunged at her. He came so close that he ripped off her face mask, the tusks missing her face by a fraction of an inch.

The hippo then attacked Alan and gored a hole in his leg. Alan recovered in a hospital in Kenya. Then he returned to filming at Mzima—but this time behind the protection of an underwater blind.

Crime-Fighting Hippos

Hippos are so unpredictable that it is hard to believe that anyone would *want* to have them around. In one village in South Africa, however, the villagers liked their hippos and fought to keep them.

For years, Khula Village was visited by a group of eight hippos. During the day, the hippos stayed in the lake. At night, they grazed right beside the homes in the village.

One night in March 2002, a young man was walking home from a soccer game. He made it no farther than Khula Village, where a hippo attacked him. The hippo gored the young man in the upper back. The man's spinal cord was damaged and his neck was dislocated. The doctors managed to save his life, but he is paralyzed from the neck down. The young man wanted the hippos killed. "I think they will attack other people,"[14] he said.

Game officials offered to destroy the hippo. The village chief replied, "This is our animal, it has lived here for more than 10 years. We do not want to have it killed."[15]

The chief explained that the hippos "were here when we first arrived in 1993 after we were moved from the Dukuduku forest. We have always enjoyed living with the animals."[16]

A face-to-face encounter with a hippo can be both frightening and dangerous.

The chief claimed that the hippos helped the village reduce crime. "Our hippos have been our security system. No one dares go out at night to commit crimes because they could become victim to our 'security force.'"[17]

Reaching a Compromise

The injured man's family pressured the chief to do something about the hippos. So they agreed on a compromise. The hippos were captured and sold at an auction for forty-one hundred dollars each. The money from the auction went to pay for the capture of the hippos, as well as to the injured man and his family.

Captive hippos enjoy an afternoon shower. Moving troublesome hippos from the wild into protected areas is an alternative to killing the animals.

The two brothers who bought the hippos own a huge game sanctuary with a man-made lake. They were delighted with their purchase. They had been trying to buy some hippos for years.

"There Are Limits"

Villagers who contend with hippos as neighbors must try to find ways to live with the unpredictable animals.

The African country of Niger had a problem with hippos in October 2000. Herds of hippos came from Mali, a country right beside Niger. The hippos were causing trouble in Mali, so the residents chased the hippos into Niger.

The hippos came down the Niger River. They smashed about a dozen boats. They also damaged the rice fields. Villagers tried to protect the rice fields by arming themselves with clubs and burning torches, but they could not stop the hippos.

The government of Niger ordered that all aggressive hippos were to be killed. "There are limits," said a government administrator. "We cannot put humans in danger under the **pretext** of wanting to protect the animals." [18]

In Niger, the government decided that killing the troublesome hippos was the most sensible solution. In some other African countries, however, killing hippos is not an option.

Tribal warriors surround a recently killed hippo during a traditional ceremony in Kenya.

The King's Hippos

The rural area of eastern Swaziland has many wetland pools where herds of hippos live. One hippo wandered from its usual habitat, as hippopotamuses sometimes do. It visited the farms near the village and devoured the crops.

In this country, the villagers do not have the option of killing the hippo. In Swaziland, all wild animals are the property of the king of Swaziland. Anyone who kills a hippo must pay a large fine, buy a new hippo to replace the old one, and spend twenty years in jail.

Night after night, the hippo ate the farmers' crops. The frustrated villagers threw stones at the hippo. The hippo tried to escape by hiding out in a pool. The villagers surrounded the pool and continued to pelt the hippo with stones whenever it showed itself. This went on for several days.

One night, one of the women in the village was returning home from a party late at night. She stumbled into the hippo in the dark. The hippo attacked quickly and viciously. The woman had to be rushed to the hospital with a gash in her leg, but she recovered.

Hippo Solutions

In these areas, the parks department may relocate a hippo. Capturing a hippo takes a long time. Tranquilizer darts cannot be used, because the hippo would then go into the water and drown. The park officials put an electric fence around hippo territory. Then they put food in a cage and wait for the hippo to go into the cage.

The head of the Big Game Parks of Swaziland also has a solution to the problem of hippos eating farmers' crops. The strategy uses one of the hippos' weaknesses: They cannot jump.

The answer, he says, is a simple fence with "a single strand of electrified wire and a well-maintained second wire at knee height. This will keep any hippo out."[19]

Since humans and hippos share common territory in certain parts of Africa, there will continue to be encounters, attacks, and the need for solutions.

Notes

Chapter 2: Encounters in Water

1. Paul Templer, "Paul Templer's Story." www.zz am.org.
2. Chris Walton, "Kayaking to 'The Spot,'" Day Twenty-Eight of "The River Journal" at www. zzam.org.
3. Richard Bangs, *Richard Bangs: Adventure Without End.* Seattle, WA: Mountaineers Books, 2001.
4. Bangs, *Richard Bangs.*
5. Bangs, *Richard Bangs.*
6. Bangs, *Richard Bangs.*
7. Bangs, *Richard Bangs.*
8. Bangs, *Richard Bangs.*
9. Bangs, *Richard Bangs.*

Chapter 3: Encounters on Land

10. Sandy Dacombe, "Mvuu," www.onafrica.net, November 13, 2000. www.onafrica.net.
11. Dacombe, "Mvuu."
12. Quoted in "Hippo Attacks Tourist," *Daily News,* Zimbabwe, June 22, 2001. www.dailynews.co.zw.

Chapter 4: Dealing with Hippos

13. Quoted in Michael Jenkinson, *Beyond the Fire: True Encounters with Man-Killing Denizens of the Sea.* New York: E.P. Dutton, 1980, pp. 84–85.

14. Quoted in Prega Govender, "Villagers Defend Crime-Fighting Hippos," *South Africa Sunday Times*, March 17, 2002.
15. Quoted in Niki Moore, "Villagers Back Rogue Hippo," *Natal Witness*, March 12, 2002. www.news 24.co.za.
16. Quoted in Govender, "Villagers Defend Crime-Fighting Hippos."
17. Quoted in Moore, "Villagers Back Rogue Hippo."
18. Quoted in "Hippos on Rampage Down Niger," *Namibian*, October 17, 2000. www.namibian. com.na.
19. Quoted in James Hall, "Endangered African Hippo Stands Its Ground," Inter Press Service, February 5, 2002. http://forests.org.

Glossary

aggravating: Making an animal more angry and more likely to attack.

amphibious: Able to live both on land and in water. From the Greek *amphibios,* meaning "living a double life."

canine: The pointed tooth just in front of the first molar (molars are the chewing teeth at the back).

channel: A narrow body of water connecting two larger bodies of water.

dominant male: The animal who commands and controls the others.

formidable: Hard to overcome.

habitat: The place where an animal normally lives.

pretext: What someone states to be their intention or aim.

prosthetic: An artificial device to replace a missing part of the body.

provoked: Stirred to action; to provoke a fight means to try to start a fight.

rogue: A destructive, bad-tempered wild animal that lives alone.

safari: An expedition, especially in Africa.

territorial: A territorial animal defends the area where it lives.

For Further Exploration

Books

Caroline Arnold, *Hippo*. New York: Morrow Junior Books, 1989. This informative book follows baby hippo Doodles and his parents, Cuddles and Puddles, at the San Francisco Zoo in California. Beautiful color photos complement the text.

Beth Wagner Brust, *Hippos*. Mankato, MN: Creative Education, 1989. Photos and illustrations show how hippos swim and fight as well as how to make a model hippo from clay.

Sigmund A. Lavine, *Wonders of Hippos*. Toronto: McLelland and Stewart, 1983. Covers hippo history and behavior as well as the hippo in art and literature.

Bradley Smith, *The Life of the Hippopotamus*. New York: World, 1972. Lots of photos by the author, including close-ups of the famous "yawn" threat and a newborn calf with its mother.

Websites

Creature Feature (www.nationalgeographic.com). Scroll down to "For Kids." Under "More Animals," select "Hippos" and press "Go." Watch a video of hippo cows and their babies, listen to hippo noises, send a hippo postcard, and more.

Hippo Dipping (http://magma.nationalgeographic.com). Choose the November 2001 issue and scroll down to "Hippo Dipping" in the center. Among the treasures from Kenya's Mzima Springs is a great video, "Fish-Powered Toothbrush."

Hippo Skull (www.geobop.com). Get a good look at those fantastic tusks in a photo of a hippopotamus skull. There is also a short description of what hippos look like: "fat-headed pigs."

Hippo Takes a Dip in Lodge's Pool (http://europe.cnn.com). See a short video of a hippo in a swimming pool while the surprised guests look on.

Toledo Zoo (http://toledo.com). A great opportunity to see hippos moving underwater in this video from the zoo in Toledo, Ohio. Includes the underwater birth of a baby hippo.

Internet Sources

Sandy Dacombe, "Mvuu," Africa on Safari, Nov. 13, 2000. www.onafrica.net

British Broadcasting Corporation, "Hippo Is Whale's Cousin." http://news.bbc.co.uk.

David Rogers, "Adrift in Time," Getaway, October 1997. www.getawaytoafrica.com.

Index

herds, 8, 10
Hippopotamus amphibius, 5

Kenya, 35
Khula Village (South Africa), 36–38

Malawi, 26–27
males
  dominant, 8, 10
  rogue, 10–11, 15–16, 18
Mali, 38–39
Mesdre, Jordi, 27–28
Mkombe, Jamaica, 28–30
mothers, 11, 27–28, 30–31
Mzima Springs (Kenya), 35

name, 5
Niger, 38–39

predators, 6

Rempler, Paul, 13, 15–16, 18–19
rogue hippos, 10–11, 15–16, 18
Root, Alan, 35
Root, Joan, 35
running ability, 7

safaris, 12
size, 6
sleeping, 8
South Africa, 28–30, 36–38
speed, 7
Swaziland, 40–41

territories, 8, 10, 11

weapons, 6

Zambezi River, 13, 15–16, 18–19, 34–35
Zimbabwe, 27–28